52

THINGS TO DO IN HAMILTON

52 THINGS TO DO IN HAMILTON

THE INSIDER'S GUIDE TO FUN IN THE HAMMER

JASON A. ALLEN

Published by James Street North Books
an imprint of Wolsak and Wynn Publishers
280 James Street North
Hamilton, ON L8R2L3
www.wolsakandwynn.ca

Editor: Noelle Allen | Copy editor: Anthony Nijssen
Cover and interior design: Jennifer Rawlinson
Author photograph: Jeff Tessier
Typeset in Metronic Slab, Hoss Round Slab and Adobe Caslon
Printed by Brant Service Press Ltd., Brantford, Canada

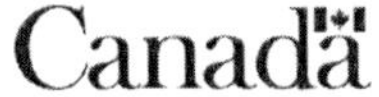

The publisher gratefully acknowledges the support of the Canada Council for the Arts and the Ontario Arts Council. We also acknowledge the financial support of the Government of Canada through the Canada Book Fund and the Government of Ontario through the Ontario Book Publishing Tax Credit and Ontario Creates.

Library and Archives Canada Cataloguing in Publication

Title: 52 things to do in Hamilton : the insider's guide to fun in the Hammer / Jason A. Allen.
Names: Allen, Jason A., author.
Identifiers: Canadiana 20250324334 | ISBN 9781998408313 (softcover)
Subjects: LCSH: Hamilton (Ont.)—Guidebooks. | LCGFT: Guidebooks.
Classification: LCC FC3098.18 .A45 2025 | DDC 917.13/52045—dc23

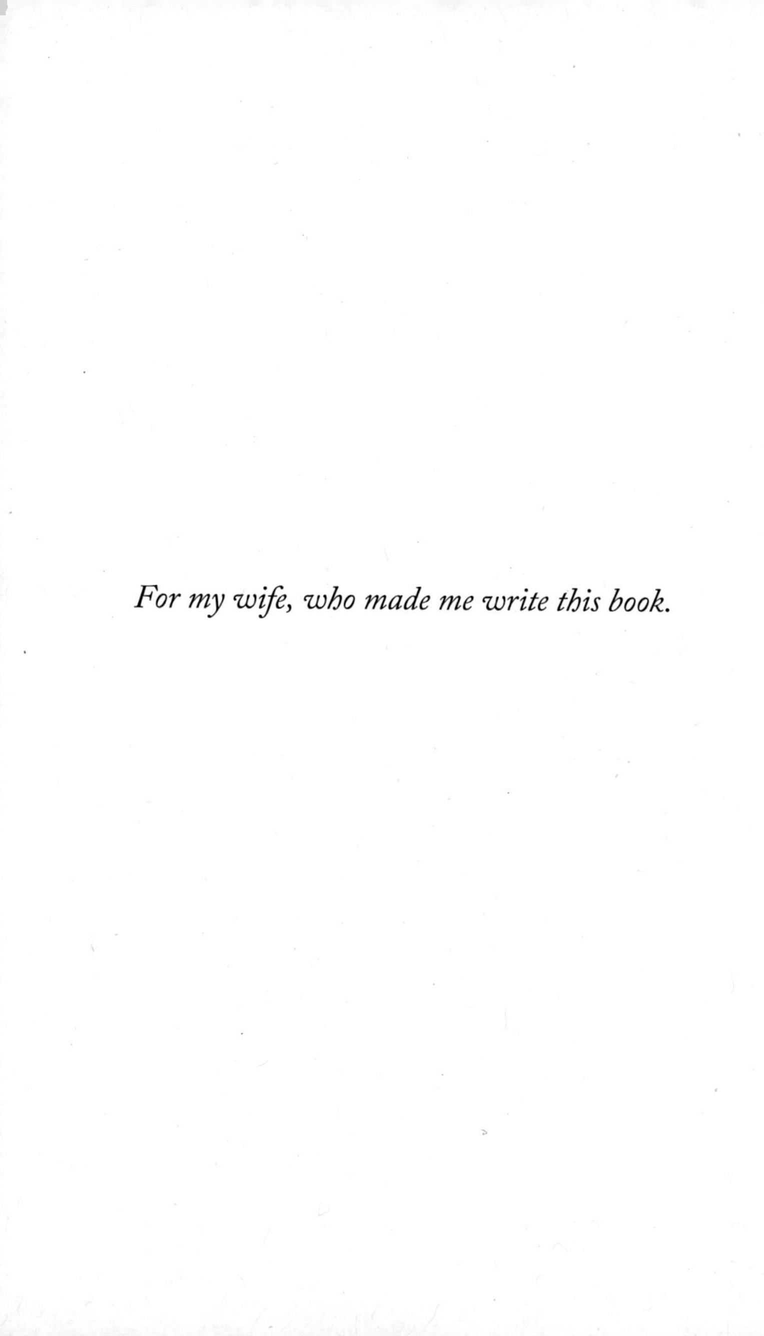

For my wife, who made me write this book.

CONTENTS

SUMMER

FALL

HOLIDAYS

INTRODUCTION

When we first moved to Ontario in 2000 from southern Alberta, my wife and I settled briefly in Guelph. We were fairly outdoorsy and were used to adventurous hikes in the Rockies, where we could go hours without seeing anyone else. Trying to get outdoors in southwest Ontario was a bit of a shock for us, as everywhere we went felt either crowded or expensive.

Then we discovered that there was a hiking trail called the Bruce Trail that ran just south of us through Hamilton and we decided to pay it a visit. We parked in a local park off York Road in Dundas, climbed the fifty or so metres of the escarpment and started on our hike. It was lush and green. A little busier than we were used to, but the views were great and the forest was full of life.

About two hours in, we realized that the only way back to our car was to backtrack our route and return the way we had come. For two experienced outdoorspeople, this was not on. One of us had the brilliant idea of bushwhacking our way down the escarpment in the hopes of connecting with York Road, which we knew was somewhere below us.

What we did not expect was a train track protected by a seven-foot-tall chain-link fence on either side. Not to be discouraged, we scaled the first fence, and – illegally I should add – crossed the tracks. After scaling the fence on the other side, we made our way to York Road, and back to our car from there.

For us, from the very beginning, Hamilton has always been about unexpected discoveries like this one. Ever since we moved to the city, five years after that fateful hiking trip, we have looked at our time in Hamilton as a big adventure, punctuated by a series of smaller adventures. Riding a miniature steam train around an elevated track with our over-the-top-excited eight-year-old? Adventure. Taking our youngest to the Festival of Friends midway so Dad's wallet can get cleaned out on games of chance? Adventure. Canoeing Cootes Paradise and startling bald eagles out of the trees? Adventure.

Hamilton is full of fascinating places and events, big and small, and the city is big enough, creative enough and diverse enough that there is something for pretty much everyone. Is your idea of a great time seeing your teen idol play their biggest hit for free in a gorgeous park? We've got you covered. Is it the crack of the bat as the home team hits one over the outfield wall? We've got that too. Is it swimming in one of the world's largest freshwater lakes before grabbing a foot-long hot dog? We can also make that happen.

Maybe your idea of fun is a hike that doesn't involve scaling seven-foot-tall chain-link fences, but still has stunning views? The city can provide that too, as I discovered after that early scramble.

This book is the product of twenty years of exploring the city we have called home and have come to love more than any of the half-dozen other places we have lived. I'm confident you can find the right kind of adventure in these pages, whether it's for you on your own, with a group of friends on a Saturday night, with fussy kids bored of summer break or with your retired partner of forty years looking for something stimulating and enriching.

This is the book I wish we'd had twenty years ago, and that I hope will take you on all sorts of adventures now. Come with me and discover a Hamilton that few outside the city know exists, and fewer still will ever get to see.

Ready? Let's go!

WINTER

Winter feels like a time to put on your fuzziest socks, pour a cup of the strongest tea and curl up with a streaming show binge or your favourite book. But you'll be missing out on an awful lot of what Hamilton has to offer if you don't get out of the house once in a while.

Winter in Hamilton – compared to a lot of Canadian cities – really isn't that cold or snowy, so there's no excuse not to come outside and play, either in nature or in any of the amazing cultural places we have here.

Keep your fuzzy socks on, but trade the slippers for boots, skates, runners or dancing shoes, and get ready to see what Hamilton can show you in the coldest months of the year.

POLAR BEAR DIP

In 1920, a Greek restaurant owner in Vancouver named Peter Pantages waded into the icy waters of the north Pacific on January first and started a tradition of polar bear dips that has spread around the world.

Hamilton is an eager participant in this brave, chilly New Year's Day adventure.

Each year, a crowd gathers at 1:00 p.m. at Van Wagner's Beach right behind Hutch's on the Beach to steel themselves for the run into the water – and the run back out to waiting towels and winter coats.

In the past it was a formally organized event,

with sponsors and prizes, often raising funds for local charity events.

However, the cost and necessity of good insurance caught up with them. The event is now widely participated in but not formally organized by anyone, in the most Hamilton way possible. There is a Facebook group where participants share photos and inspiration, but that's the extent of the organizing.

Despite the popularity in recent years of cold plunges and their touted health benefits, that's not the reason most plungers are out there. In Hamilton, participants cite things like tradition, courage and just plain fun for their annual run into the not quite frozen lake.

Photos from the event show participants from young people all the way up to seniors in their seventies and eighties. People run into the water wearing everything from tiny Speedos to mermaid and *Braveheart* costumes, to Ticats and Hamilton Forge jerseys. They come from all walks of life and in all shapes and sizes, united in their desire to get really, really cold for just a few moments, and then delightfully warm again afterwards.

Even if you don't want to go into the water, going down to the event to cheer on a friend or stranger can be a fun way to welcome in the new year and get things off to a lighthearted start.

Van Wagner's Beach is located just north of the QEW at Centennial Parkway. Exit at the Parkway and turn left onto Van Wagners Beach Road/North Service Road and drive until you see the Hutch's parking lot. There is no transit service there in the winter, but plenty of parking if you're carpooling or driving.

ART GALLERY OF HAMILTON (AGH)

If you're looking for an indoor activity that will broaden your horizons and expose you to something new and beautiful, you can't do much better than the Art Gallery of Hamilton.

This award-winning gallery, with its collection of over ten thousand items, is right downtown on King Street. The gallery features regular touring exhibits, many of which only have one or two stops in Canada, meaning the AGH is often the only place in Ontario to see them. In the past, these exhibitions have featured themes such as surrealism, reflections on growing up Muslim and Indigenous artwork.

While the travelling exhibitions are world class, the AGH's permanent collection is no less impressive. Featuring works from artists such as Alex Colville, the Group of Seven, Emily Carr, James Tissot, Kim Adams and Edward Burtynsky, it's a collection of world-renowned artists you won't find anywhere else.

The AGH also offers a wide variety of programming for all ages. Whether it's the regular talks and tours of their exhibitions, the Seniors Connect sessions that bring seniors together to explore themes in art or the Youth Arts Collective, the AGH appeals to a broad range of interests.

The gallery is located at 123 King Street West, across from the Sheraton Hotel. There is parking off of Summers Lane near the main entrance, and the area is well served by many Hamilton Street Railway (HSR) routes, with the Frank A. Cooke Transit Terminal only a five-minute walk away.

The gallery is open Thursday to Sunday, and Thursday is free admission all day, making it a great deal for those looking to save a few dollars and still be able to take in amazing art. Students also receive free admission throughout the week, and there are admission discounts for seniors on the other days.

Check out their website at www.artgalleryof

hamilton.com for more details and to plan your visit to this treasure trove of art in downtown Hamilton.

MCMASTER BASKETBALL

Hamilton has long been a hot spot for great basketball, producing players such as Kia Nurse and Shai Gilgeous-Alexander. However, our short-lived professional club, the Honey Badgers, moved to Brampton due to the renovations of the downtown arena. This loss gives us a golden opportunity to highlight our amateur athletes.

The McMaster basketball program is an excellent choice if you want to catch some great ball on a winter's evening. The women's team were national champions in 2019, and while it's been a bit longer since the men's team won a provincial championship, both teams continue to field excellent players year after year.

The games are played in the 2,250-seat Burridge Gymnasium, located in the David Braley Athletic Centre. The gym features concessions and accessible washrooms, and is often a noisy and fun place when the team gets going.

The season runs from August, with the first game usually just before university classes resume, to the end of February, when the first round of playoffs begins. Home games are generally two to three times a month. Watch for doubleheaders and special events like Pride Night celebrating the 2SLGBTQIA+ community and players.

Tickets for a game are quite reasonable, running $12 for adults, $5 for youth aged 12–17, and free for kids under 12 and currently enrolled McMaster students.

The David Braley Athletic Centre is located on the McMaster campus. There is plenty of parking available, but it's expensive. Several HSR routes stop nearby, including the 01 and the 05. Do not park in Westdale and walk, as the one-hour limit on parking in that neighbourhood is strictly enforced. You will get a ticket.

SHARP WORDS: HAMILTON'S WINTER BOOK FAIR

In late January, Hamilton book lovers come together for their favourite event of the winter: an adult version of a Scholastic book fair. That is, if it had been organized by the cool kids in school who listened to campus radio.

That's right, it's the annual Sharp Words Winter Book Fair.

Each year, a collection of independent Canadian-owned publishing companies and local authors gather to give you a great selection of small press books, chapbooks, zines, indie magazines and comics.

These are books you often won't find at a big

chain bookstore, published by small presses, which often run on caffeine and dedication. It's the perfect place to browse for something new and fresh, and to talk to the people who made that book, comic or chapbook happen.

But it's not just a book fair; there is an afternoon's worth of engaging panel discussions with authors, publishers, media personalities and activists from Hamilton and the surrounding area. They discuss things like trends in writing and publishing, how to get published and the topics that keep writers and industry experts on their toes.

One of the biggest highlights of the day, though, is the literary cabaret that caps off the evening. In its first year, a group of musicians gathered to offer a unique form of entertainment: live band karaoke, with the singing done by authors and members of Hamilton's literary community.

It was such a hit that the band took on the name The Approximators and have since continued to play their live karaoke show at bars and events around southern Ontario. Now they're the official after-party.

Sharp Words happens at the Bridgeworks venue near Barton and Bay Streets, and while there is ample parking, it's a little tough to get to without a car. The nearest transit stop is at the corner of

Cannon and Hess Streets, served by HSR route 08. From there it's a short walk up Caroline Street and through the park to get there.

Make this the year you scratch that itch for some reading material that's a little out of the ordinary, and head down to Sharp Words!

TOBOGGANING

Winter for many families with kids means making the most of the outdoors and getting the little ones into the fresh air as much as possible. And what winter outdoor activity is more iconic than tobogganing?

The history of the activity in Hamilton is a little fraught, as a number of years ago someone was injured on a hill and sued the city. The legislators at City Hall responded by banning the practice everywhere, until the public outcry became too great.

Now, Hamilton has joined a number of other cities in Ontario to create official tobogganing hills where you can go when your kids feel the need for winter speed. The two of the most iconic are the hills at the Garth and Stone Church reservoir and Chedoke Golf Club.

The reservoir hills are short, but very steep, so you can get a good head of steam going. In the interest of safety, the city places a row of wrapped straw bales along the base of the hill where it meets the sidewalk to prevent sledders from flying out onto a busy road. You would have to have a very fast sled, or multiple people on a sled, to hit the bales very hard, but always exercise caution.

At Chedoke Golf Club, the hill is just off the parking lot, and is long, steep and fairly fast. Be sure to watch out for the trees that line the edges of the run. If you've got a good sled, be prepared for a long trudge up the hill from the golf course. The bonus here, of course, is the restaurant/café at the top of the hill, which is open some weekends for sledders to enjoy a hot chocolate and use the washrooms. The restaurant changes hands and names periodically, so search online for details.

Other hills include a gentler slope at the Dundas Driving Park, as well as King's Forest Golf Club in the east end. The Dundas Driving Park also features a regularly groomed skating rink with change rooms and a concession stand, letting you double your winter fun.

Grab a thermos of hot chocolate, your best sled and some head protection, and get ready for an afternoon of wintry fun on one of Hamilton's officially sanctioned toboggan hills.

HAMILTON WINTERFEST

Winter can be the hardest time to get out of your cozy nest and face the world. Days are short, weather can be unpredictable and making plans seems like inviting disappointment.

The good people who organize Hamilton Winterfest every year have a solution for all that: a two week–long festival at the beginning of February with so much to see and do there's no reason to stay home.

The main event moves locations once in a while, but for the last few years it has been at Jackson Square downtown, where offerings have included art installations, live concerts, aerial shows and other fun and games suitable for the whole family.

While some parts of the festival are ticketed, much of it is free. This includes the rooftop concerts, which always draw a big crowd to the huge, tragically underused space on top of our downtown mall.

Beyond the main events there is even more to see and do. Much of the city gets involved in one way or another, with events taking place at many city-run locations such as libraries and civic museums. Cultural institutions also often participate, with the AGH, McMaster University and various sports teams featuring everything from special art gallery exhibits to charity hockey games and planetarium shows.

With so much going on, how could you possibly keep track?

Good news! The website (www.hamilton winterfest.ca) has all the details on all the events affiliated with the festival, whether they are being put on by the organizers – Cobalt Connects – or another community group. There you can also find details of ticketed events, a comprehensive calendar, bios and details of artists and performers, and maps to guide your way to the various venues.

So lace up your boots and get out and enjoy some of Hamilton's most rewarding cultural offerings at Hamilton Winterfest.

PLANETARIUM

Hidden in the depths of the Burke Science Building on the McMaster campus is a tiny, perfect jewel of a room that will let you zoom out of your seat at light speed and explore the cosmos. I'm talking about the W.J. McCallion Planetarium, one of Hamilton's best kept secrets and a fun destination for all ages.

This planetarium was the first in Ontario to offer shows to the general public. The original projector was purchased in 1949 and initially operated in another location using a WWII surplus parachute as a ceiling. It moved into its current room in 1954, and the projector received a significant upgrade to a fully digital system in 2024.

Shows are about an hour long and vary by time of year and the scheduled programming. There is always a general show, usually hosted by an astronomy or astrophysics graduate student, that provides a wonderful romp through the solar system, the constellations and even intergalactic space. Instructors are knowledgeable and often able to field a variety of questions from curious audiences.

There are also specialty shows throughout the year. In the past, these have included Indigenous star stories, a look at comets and asteroids and the ancient astronomy of Earth's first scientists.

A full schedule is available on their website: planetarium.physics.mcmaster.ca.

Public shows are Wednesdays and some Saturdays, and generally cost less than $10 a ticket. Private shows are sold based on booking the whole room (capacity thirty-five people) and are available almost any time during the week before 8:00 p.m. and on weekends before 7:00 p.m. These are an excellent value for school and community groups that want an engaging activity for their youth.

They have also hosted anniversaries, birthday parties and even wedding proposals! Anything goes for the science lover in your life.

Parking isn't ideal for this location. There are

two lots nearby, but they can be expensive. This is one of those cases where carpooling or taking transit really is a better option. The campus is served by a number of HSR routes, and most of them stop a hundred-metre walk from the Burke Science Building.

Avoid parking in Westdale and walking, as parking near the campus is limited to one hour and is quite strictly enforced.

The W.J. McCallion Planetarium is a great way for the science aficionado in your life to learn more about the stars and planets, and explore the wonders of the night sky. It's also a creative way to occupy your kid who is constantly full of questions for an hour. Either way, it's one of Hamilton's hidden gems you and your family will want to explore.

SKATING AT PRINCESS POINT

There are some things that are just quintessentially Canadian: pouring fresh, hot maple syrup on snow and eating it; complaining about the weather; wearing flannel and, of course, skating on a frozen pond.

In Hamilton, we are very fortunate to have a large, shallow pond – or wetland as it were – called Cootes Paradise. The advantage of it being shallow is that, in winter, it is one of the first bodies of water to freeze thick enough (ten centimetres at least!) to safely walk or skate on.

Long before ice fishing opens at Valens Lake, or it's safe to walk on the bay, a frozen Cootes

Paradise welcomes skaters of all ages and abilities.

This is strictly a do-it-yourself affair. The Royal Botanical Gardens manages the area and owns the parking lot at Princess Point that you'll need to access the ice. Some years they set up concession stands and fires to warm yourself around, as well as other activities. Most years, though, they just leave it, and you can come and skate for no more than the parking fee. The area is also accessible by HSR (route 06).

That means there are no skate rentals, and in the evening no lights either, so it is strictly an at-your-own-risk outing, but there are few things as magical in winter as doing lazy circles on the ice as the sun sets over one end of the marsh and the moon rises over the other.

Always pay attention to the sign at the top of the kayak launch, which is where you'll start skating from. RBG is excellent about updating this sign with current ice conditions. You do not want to go out if the ice is less than ten centimetres thick. Not only will you get wet and possibly be in a lot of danger if you fall through, but under the ice, at the bottom of the marsh, is what can only be described as unspeakable muck. You do not want to get stuck in it.

The sign also has a map that indicates which

sections of the ice are safe, and which are not. Some parts of the marsh experience pretty constant currents, and as such the ice never really gets safe to walk on. Please pay attention and follow these warnings.

In the end, skating at Princess Point is a wonderful way to spend a sunny, crisp weekend afternoon, or to head out after work one evening to stretch out some kinks on the ice. Just be safe, and you'll make memories that last forever.

EAST COAST KITCHEN PARTY

On a frosty night sometimes you just want to warm up with friends and have a bit of a party, and nobody knows how to party quite like folks from the East Coast.

This perhaps explains the longevity of the East Coast Kitchen Party with Ferguson Young at the Corktown Pub in Corktown.

The event has been running since 2008, featuring the same fiddle player, Hamilton prodigy Liam McGlashon. He's been performing at the Corktown and at stages around the city since he was eight years old, and the East Coast music scene in Hamilton has grown up around him.

The Corktown features a number of Celtic themed events, such as a weekly Irish dancing workshop, but the East Coast Kitchen Party is the longest running of these events and always attracts a good crowd.

That's likely because the music is great, with Liam on fiddle and usually accompanied by a guitar player/singer and a bass player.

Their sets are a blend of Irish and Celtic traditional songs, along with modern tracks from the likes of The Waterboys and Great Big Sea. And of course you'll find a whole bunch of singalongs, like "Country Roads," peppered throughout the set if you want to join in and belt one out with the crowd.

The Corktown is one of the (if not the) oldest continually operating pubs in Hamilton and has the atmosphere to prove it. Old wood and cozy tables along with solid pub grub and an expansive draft menu mean you'll have plenty to snack on and drink while the music plays.

The party runs Friday evenings from 6:30 to 8:30 p.m., and in the winter, you're probably going to want to make reservations by calling the Corktown in advance at 905-572-9242.

The Corktown is located in the historic Corktown neighbourhood, just east of downtown, at 175 Young Street. Parking is available in the Corktown's parking lot, or around the corner on Ferguson Avenue. You can also get there by HSR route 05 or 01 along Main Street. The pub is about a ten-minute walk south from the Main and Walnut stop through a tunnel under the train tracks. Please don't drink and drive.

SPRING

Spring is a time of hope and renewal. In many cultures we celebrate the coming of more light, more green and more warmth. In Hamilton, we also celebrate architecture, history and things that explode in the sky!

Get ready to step out in style and learn about the fascinating past of our city, and feel not only the spring sun on your face but the spring in your step as you get ready to take in all this city has to offer.

WESTFIELD HERITAGE VILLAGE

There is no better way to spend some time in the spring than enjoying the taste of fresh maple syrup, and if you would like a taste of history to go along with it, you can't beat an afternoon at Westfield Heritage Village.

Westfield is a historic re-enactment of a village of early Ontario settlers, with buildings dating from the late 1800s. It includes a blacksmith shop, a printing press, a one-room schoolhouse, a pre-Confederation trading post and a general store.

One of the most dramatic features of the village is the Toronto, Hamilton and Buffalo Railway steam locomotive parked on the grounds with the historic train station right next to it. At various times of the year you can explore the station, and at Christmas you can even send Morse code messages by telegraph to Santa!

These buildings are regularly staffed by volunteer interpreters in period costume who are thoroughly knowledgeable about the time period and activities they are re-enacting.

The village is perfect for wandering from building to building and soaking in the history of our country right around the time it became a country. On special occasions, period actors roam the grounds, interacting with visitors and providing an educational and entertaining flair to the visit.

Every spring, the village transforms into a huge sugaring-off festival, with fires and cauldrons of maple sap boiling in the village square, and a sugar shack set up just a short walk into the sugar bush just outside of town along the appropriately named Sugar Shack Trail.

In the spring, summer and fall, Westfield's trails behind the town are another Hamilton hidden gem, carpeted by spring ephemerals just after the snow melts and offering stunning fall colours later in the year. There are even ruins to be spotted along the way for those with sharp eyes and a desire to explore.

There is ample parking at Westfield, but it is not accessible by transit. Admission is set by the Hamilton Conservation Authority, which manages the site, and general admission is included in your annual HCA Membership Pass if you have one. Admission to special events like the sugaring-off and the holiday events are usually included with your pass, but need to be booked in advance online, which is subject to an extra fee.

REPERTORY CINEMAS

Some spring days are the early warm sun on your face and flowers and budding trees. Other spring days are wet rain and that cold that sinks into your bones and won't let go. For days like that, it's good to get indoors and find your entertainment there.

Those who love film, speaker series and live music are in luck. Hamilton is fortunate enough to have two fantastic repertory cinemas: The Westdale and the Playhouse Cinema.

The Westdale is a historic theatre at 1014 King Street West that has a wide range of shows and programming. At its core, it's an art house movie cinema that shows the best of independent movies from around the world. It also shows more mainstream movies and truly plays a role as a local theatre surrounded by plenty of great places to eat and get a coffee.

Be sure to catch a Film Talk when a great movie is scheduled. These periodic events feature people involved with the production of the film coming to give viewers the inside scoop on how it was made, and what happened along the way.

The Westdale also has plenty of live music and theatre in its luxurious red-seated room that holds about 340 people. Concessions there sell your usual popcorn and candy, along with beer and wine for those old enough to take part.

There is parking in front of the theatre or along King Street, but don't park in the neighbourhood, as you'll get a ticket if you're there more than an hour. You can also catch HSR routes 01 or 05, which stop about fifty metres from the front door at King and Marion.

Meanwhile, over in the east end, the Playhouse Cinema brings authentic rep cinema to the border of the steadily revitalizing Barton Village. It also features a wide range of movies, some of which are hard to find in theatres, and an extensive series of speakers and live events.

The cinema also runs a number of specialty

series throughout the year, including holiday favourites, horror classics and rare showings of movies on 35mm film on the lovingly restored projector.

There aren't as many places to eat or get coffee near the Playhouse, except for Pinch Bakery and Plant Shop next door, which isn't always open at movie times. Be sure to grab a popcorn and a drink before you head in for your show.

The Playhouse is at 177 Sherman Avenue North, which is a one-way street headed north. There are fourteen parking spots beside the building for those who get there early; otherwise there is usually lots of metered street parking along Barton. HSR route 02 (the fabled Wonderbus) also stops a few steps away from the Playhouse at Barton Street and Sherman Avenue.

HMCS *HAIDA*

Canada's modern military history is in large part a naval history, largely by virtue of where Canada is located compared to where most conflicts happen, and there is no part of our naval history quite as celebrated as the HMCS *Haida*, Canada's "most fightingest warship."

The good news, for those who love exploring that history, is that the *Haida* is now a national historic site located at Pier 9 in Hamilton's bayfront. Here, visitors can explore the ship, take part in interpretive tours and participate in events to commemorate the ship that take place throughout the year.

The *Haida* is the sole survivor of the twenty-seven Tribal-class destroyers that were built. It operated around the world during World War II, the Korean War and the Cold War. Originally deployed during World War II in the Arctic running supplies to Russia, the *Haida* distinguished itself in battle in the English Channel, where it effected a daring rescue of crew from a sunken fellow destroyer.

In 1963, the ship was decommissioned, having travelled almost 700,000 nautical miles in a storied career. It was rescued from the scrap heap by a private organization that paid to retrofit it and restore it as a historical site. It was docked in Hamilton in 2003 where it has remained ever since.

Daily activities at the ship include a main deck guided tour and an "action stations" tour. There is also a battle map program that takes place on the jetty before going on board. The *Haida* is also involved in programs throughout the year, including memorial services, Sea Cadet programming and historical commemorations. The *Haida*'s website includes a calendar of events that has all of the details and can be found at parks.canada.ca/lhn-nhs/on/haida.

The *Haida* is easily accessible by car, and there is ample parking all around it at Pier 9. It can also be accessed via transit from HSR route 20 if you don't mind a bit of a walk. There are admission discounts for seniors, while youth 17 and under can visit for free. The site is also included as part of the Parks Canada Discovery Pass (parkscanadashop .ca/pages/discovery-pass).

RAPTOR MIGRATION

The Iroquoia Heights Conservation Area is a hidden gem located on the west mountain, just at the border with Ancaster. This natural area used to be the route of an electric tram that ran from Hamilton to Brantford. The rail trail that runs right though the conservation area's heart is a smooth, gravel footpath that easily accommodates bicycles, strollers and even wheelchairs.

From the main trail, you can see the white rectangular blazes (paint used to mark trails) on trees and posts of the Bruce Trail that runs from Niagara Falls to the tip of Tobermory at the furthest northern part of southern Ontario.

Hamilton's slice of the Bruce Trail runs through some of the most unspoiled nature in the city, and the stretch through Iroquoia Heights is no exception.

The conservation area is a treat any time of year, but the moment when it really shines is early to mid-spring when the raptors are migrating from their winter homes in the United States to their summer homes further north. The escarpment provides the perfect corridor for them.

Some raptors, such as hawks and vultures, hunt by floating in the air and scanning the ground below for motion (in the case of hawks) or the scent of something decomposing (in the case of vultures). Either way, it is in the raptors' best interests to use as little energy as possible when hunting, and the air currents along the escarpment provide the perfect opportunity for this. As the air at the base of the escarpment heats up, it rises quickly up the cliff face, forming thermal updrafts that lift the raptors up and allow them to soar effortlessly above the ground.

It's a thrilling sight every spring, and there is no better place in Hamilton to watch this than Iroquoia Heights.

From the parking lot on Scenic Drive at the north end of the hydro corridor, head west across the paved trail onto the gravel rail trail. Just past the sound of Chedoke Falls on the right, you'll see two white blazes and a set of stairs leading down into the woods. Follow these for the trail toward the edge of the escarpment.

From here, caution is key, because at several points along the trail, the fence has been broken and you can access the very edge of the cliff. Without putting yourself in danger, you can stand just inside the broken fence at several points along this trail with binoculars and watch the raptors coming up to soar at eye level in front of you.

Obviously, dogs need to be kept on a leash and little ones need to be closely watched, but if you love big birds with sharp beaks and talons and want to get as close as you can in nature, there is no better time than during the spring raptor migration at Iroquoia Heights Conservation Area.

FORGE FC

Did you know that Hamilton has its very own – very successful – team in the most popular sport in the world? Nope, it's not baseball (although we have a great baseball team), or NFL football (although we also have a well-loved Canadian Football League team). It's the other football, soccer, and Hamilton's Forge FC is one of the best teams in Canada.

Formed in 2017 as part of the newly created Canadian Premier League, Forge FC joined teams from across Canada to form Canada's professional soccer league, a league it has pretty much dominated ever since.

Forge FC won league championships in 2019, 2020, 2022 and 2023, and has also played internationally at the CONCACAF Champions league level against teams from across the United States and Mexico.

Forge FC games in Hamilton are played at Hamilton Stadium and are a real family affair. The season starts in April, and the stands fill with people in their bright orange jerseys and hats. If you have anything orange to wear, this is the place to do it!

Games can vary quite a bit in terms of non-soccer activities. Some games are just a chance to hang out with friends, enjoy a beverage in the sunshine and watch some really great soccer. Other games have fun activities geared toward the whole family. These have included bouncy castles, on field chances to kick goals, barbecues and visits with Sparx, the team mascot.

Forge FC crowds are known for being particularly enthusiastic, and because the attendance is smaller than a Ticat game, they only open one side of the stadium (the sunny side) for fans to sit in.

If you're planning on attending, especially with kids, make sure to check out their website at www.canpl.ca/forgefc for game day entertainment details.

Single game tickets run from $25 and up, with

good seats available for $50. Lineups for washrooms and concessions tend to be pretty minimal, so don't worry about missing any of the action standing in line.

Parking is usually available around the stadium either on the street, or in Stipley neighbourhood residents' driveways for a small fee; look for the handmade signs. The stadium is also easily accessible by HSR along Cannon (route 03) and King Streets (routes 01 and 10).

AROUND THE BAY ROAD RACE

Ready to lace up your runners for a quick run? Maybe a long run? Maybe a long-running long run? The Around the Bay Road Race may be just the thing for you.

As the oldest running race in North America, people have been running, jogging and briskly walking sections of this route since 1894. When it was first conceived by local cigar store owner Billy Carroll, it ran on Christmas Day that year, three years before the first Boston Marathon.

Originally a men's-only race, a woman named Tersilla Komac challenged the establishment in 1975 by just showing up and running it unofficially.

She was registered the next year by a friend using just her first initial, and finally in 1979 race organizers relented and opened it up to everyone.

The race itself was cancelled in 2020 during the height of the pandemic, and run virtually the following year, but it is now back in all its glory, testing the might and mettle of people who come from around the world to run its length.

The thirty-kilometre route currently runs from just north of LIUNA Station, down along Burlington Street, out along the water on Beach Boulevard, then back along North Shore Boulevard to York Boulevard and ending downtown.

The event features a 10K race, a longer 15K race and, of course, the full 30K route.

The route itself is steeped in history, with many parts of the route now the stuff of legend.

The start of the race is a glorious mob of enthusiastic runners heading out in the crisp spring air on their way to claim victory. It makes for a great photograph.

Then be prepared to struggle up Hamilton's version of Heartbreak Hill – the road up the escarpment along Valley Inn Road – and to possibly be greeted by someone dressed as the Grim Reaper at the top of the hill.

For the rest of the afternoon, you'll see flushed,

happy-looking runners all around the city sporting their finishing medals over a celebratory coffee, lunch or pint.

Of course, if running isn't for you, the race itself is powered by a small army of volunteers, who do everything from registering and checking in participants to handing out medals at the end of the run. You can also always just show up along the racecourse as a spectator to cheer people on. The race draws crowds of varying sizes depending on the weather, and runners always appreciate an encouraging cheer as they make their way along the route.

The Around the Bay Road Race is such a tradition in Hamilton that many people have run it several times, and you will often see people strapping on their shoes and starting to train as soon as the new year turns.

Will this be the year you brave the course?

GRITLIT: HAMILTON'S READERS AND WRITERS FESTIVAL

Every April, just as the creeks and rivers start to really run, Hamilton's most avid readers and writers make a run of a different kind to gritLIT: Hamilton's Readers and Writers Festival.

Started in 2004 by local writers, the event has now grown into the largest literary event in the city. Every year, the best in literary talent from around Hamilton and across the country share their works in readings, panel discussions and contests.

The readings and panels are the highlights for many attendees, where they get to hear their favourite literary stars reading from their latest works first-hand. These panels always feature a lively discussion between guests and are followed by the all-important question-and-answer period with the audience.

gritLIT is known for being one of the best places for getting up close and personal with the authors you love and it's the intimate setting and small rooms of the event that make this possible.

One of the most exciting parts of the event is the writing contest. Every year, the festival accepts short works (usually under 500 words) of fiction or creative nonfiction for consideration by an esteemed local judge. The submission page for the contest even contains helpful tips on how to craft an effective and maybe award-winning piece of writing (www.gritlit.ca/contest).

Of course, every year at the event there is a table with local bookseller Epic Books offering the books by the featured authors. Bring a sturdy bag, because you'll be going home with a number of new favourites.

While the festival is the big draw for gritLIT, the organizers also present a number of smaller events throughout the year. These events range from large theatre readings with the likes of Margaret Atwood to small intimate gatherings where people read or write in silence, enjoying the hospitality of local pubs and being surrounded by fellow literary enthusiasts.

All in all, if you love reading, and especially if you aspire to being a writer, gritLIT is the place you want to be every April.

SPRING EPHEMERALS AT THE ROYAL BOTANICAL GARDENS (RBG)

Every year the forests in and around Hamilton put on a dazzling show of colour, texture and delicacy. I'm not describing the budding spring leaves or even the deafening sound of the spring peepers here; I'm talking about the natural fireworks display that is early spring flowers, or spring ephemerals.

Over thousands of years these plants have evolved to be an early food source for native bees and other pollinators who are just waking as the ground warms up. In order to attract those early bees and insects, spring ephemerals need to put on a bit of a show, and that's just what they do. Whether it's the showy white petals of our provincial flower, the trillium, or the delicate beauty of the trout lily, you will grow to appreciate them just as much as bees do.

In Hamilton and Burlington, there is nowhere better to see these early spring flowers than the Royal Botanical Gardens' Arboretum, which is also known for its cherry blossom and lilac displays later in the spring.

Located on Old Guelph Road, most easily accessed from York Boulevard just east of the McQuesten High Level Bridge, there is ample paid parking, and usually not a lot of crowds at this time of year.

Head directly toward the magnolia grove and then down the hill toward the water. At the waterfront, head to the right and up the hill toward Bull's Point Trail. Along the wall of soil and leaves to your right is where you'll see the earliest flowers, often harbingers of spring poking their yellow heads above the sun-warmed soil a full two weeks before those in the deeper forest along Grey Doe Trail.

At any point along the trail you may spot trout lilies, trilliums, hepaticas, bloodroot or any number of other flowers. A decent online guide or guidebook will help you identify them. Some, like trout lilies and mayapples, seem to deliberately hide from view and can take keen eyes to identify. If you have kids, make it into a scavenger hunt and see how many they can spot.

That said, please. Please. Do not pick any of these flowers. Spring ephemerals are just that: ephemeral. They are not robust plants and do not do well being handled or dealt with roughly in any way. Trilliums, for example, can take a full five years to go from seed to their first flower, and even disturbing or compacting the soil around them to get a close-up photo can shorten their lives.

Use the zoom feature on your phone or bring a decent telephoto lens to get a good shot. Stepping near a flower for a better shot could mean you're stepping on – and killing – a flower that hasn't yet bloomed.

Spring ephemerals are very weather dependent, so if we're having a warm spring, you may need to get out as early as March to avoid missing them, but in colder years the display can continue well into May.

Plan to go on a warm sunny day for maximum viewing, and be sure to pack a warm drink to sit and sip in one of the red chairs or at viewpoints along the way.

I promise you won't look at spring in the forest the same way again.

HAMILTON MUSEUM OF STEAM AND TECHNOLOGY

People young and old love machines. Kids especially love them, the bigger the better. But what about a mechanical pump so big that it takes up an entire building, and was designed to pump fresh water from Lake Ontario all the way to the top of the escarpment?

We're talking about the Hamilton Museum of Steam and Technology, a monument to mid-1800s architecture, engineering and ambition.

The pump was commissioned in 1854, around the time of a cholera epidemic that killed hundreds of people in the city, and it was designed to supply fresh water for forty thousand people – four times the population of Hamilton at the time. The facility was completed in 1860 and opened by King Edward VII, then the Prince of Wales, who happened to be on a Canadian tour at the time.

The museum is still home to the two enormous steam engines and pumps that took water from the lake to a spot three kilometres away on the escarpment so it could be fed by gravity to the rest of the city below.

Now a national historic site, it is open year-round for visitors to come and visit, and maybe even try their hand at moving the enormous steel flywheels that transferred power from the steam engines to the pumps.

Every May, the museum also plays host to the Boats in the Park event held by the Confederation Marine Modellers, a group of miniature boat enthusiasts who gather to show off their hobby with interactive activities for people of all ages. In summer, the grounds also feature the Golden Horseshoe Live Steamers club on select weekends. This organization runs miniature steam locomotives that you can ride on along a track around the grounds. Get there early and be prepared to wait in line for this popular attraction.

The museum is located at 900 Woodward Avenue and there is ample parking at the site. It is also served by the HSR route 11 bus.

Hours and admission rates can be found by going to www.hamilton.ca and searching "Steam and Technology Museum." However, anyone with a physical or digital Hamilton Public Library card gets in free here and at the other City of Hamilton museums (www.hpl.ca/museum).

MOTHER'S DAY FISHING

Hamilton has an embarrassment of riches when it comes to natural areas, but you also can't forget some of our more sculpted outdoor spaces when it comes to getting outside. For places like that, you can't beat Bayfront Park.

Every spring and summer you will see anglers testing the waters around the park with a rod, reel and various baits and lures, and you may have wanted to try it too.

Good news! Every Mother's Day weekend in Ontario, you can fish waterways without the fishing licence that everyone over 18 in Ontario usually needs to have in order to enjoy the sport. This means you could head down to any number of great spots around the park to drop a line and some bait in the water and enjoy your afternoon.

You should always be sure to follow the regulations that can be found at www.ontario.ca/page/fishing, as they dictate how many fish you can take home to eat and what kind of hooks and lures you're allowed to use.

Since the harbour was cleaned up dramatically when the Randle Reef coal tar deposits were finally capped in a huge steel container in 2023, the fish in the harbour are much safer to eat. However, you should always follow Ontario ministry guidelines on how many fish from each waterway you should eat in a month.

Some of the best places around the park to fish include the small shelter and pier just to the left of the parking lot when you pull in, and the rocks and areas facing the yacht club on the opposite side of the park.

You can also walk a little ways to the north to Pier 4 Park where a long straight wall above the water near the tugboat play structure is also great for casting a line.

This is a great activity for packing a lunch or snack and some sunscreen, and spending the day enjoying the water and the sunshine. And who knows? Maybe you'll get a lucky catch.

DOORS OPEN HAMILTON

As you'd expect from a city founded in the early 1800s, Hamilton is rich with architectural treasures. In fact, we have quite a remarkable number of old buildings and homes that are still standing thanks to the dedication of an enthusiastic community of preservationists here in town.

Often we can only admire these buildings from the outside, except for once a year, in early May, when Doors Open takes place across the city.

Doors Open originated in France in 1984 and has since spread around the world. Ontario has a thriving Doors Open scene, and Hamilton's annual event usually features over fifty locations, many of which are inaccessible to the general public for the rest of the year.

These include historical treasures such as Auchmar Manor House, the legendary home of Isaac Buchanan, who was a civic leader in Hamilton in the 1800s. Other rarely open locations have included Grant Avenue Studio, a recording studio that is the source of a number of bestselling and Juno-winning albums; Tisdale House, which is the oldest home in Ancaster; and the John Lyle-designed Central Presbyterian Church.

Some locations also feature interactive exhibits, and the event usually hosts several walking tours as well. And the cost? Free, although donations are always welcome.

This event is powered by volunteers, so if you love beautiful settings and sharing what you know with strangers, perhaps consider stepping up for a shift. You'll get to spend some quality time in a building that not everyone gets a chance to see and share your love of history and architecture.

The locations, as you can imagine, are scattered throughout the city, so it's a good idea to spend some time on the website (search Doors Open Hamilton in your favourite search engine) and plan out your route and your days. The event stretches from the Museum of Steam and Technology in the east end all the way to the far west end of Ancaster, so plan your driving and be sure to bring snacks for the car!

If you love history, or great architecture, or just like to poke your nose around in places you wouldn't normally get to, Doors Open Hamilton is a must-see event for early May.

VICTORIA DAY FIREWORKS

Who doesn't love a good fireworks show? In Hamilton, there are only two weekends in the year when it is legal to set off home fireworks: the Canada Day and Victoria Day long weekends.

But who wants a little home show when you can go and see a great professional show for free? That's why on the Sunday of the Victoria Day long weekend, you want to head to Dundas Driving Park.

It's quite the celebration. They close the park to vehicles as of 7:00 a.m., but you can park at a nearby Dundas municipal lot for free and walk up the hill to the park.

Once there, you'll find entertainment for the whole family, including a music festival and a kids stage. The performers are generally all local favourites playing songs you know and love.

There will also be a row of food trucks with a variety of cuisines from around the world for sale. And finally, there will be Glow Sticks for purchase at the event, if you didn't think to bring your own.

For this event, no pets are permitted in the park, nor are you allowed to bring sparklers or fly drones, but you won't need any of that. At 9:30 p.m. or so, once twilight is over, the sky will be lit up with an exciting display of pyrotechnics set to music.

It is all put on by Rotary Club of Dundas Valley Sunrise, who host the event every year.

If you don't want to drive and fight for parking, you can catch the route 05 HSR bus there, which runs the whole length of the day and puts on extra service for the event. Check out www.hamilton.ca/home-neighbourhood/hsr for more details close to the date.

You can learn more about the fireworks display and the celebration that day by going to www.hamilton.ca and searching "Victoria Day Fireworks."

Get ready to ooh and aah with lots of new friends as the Rotary Club of Dundas Valley Sunrise lights up the night sky.

SUMMER

For most people in Hamilton, summer means one thing: festivals. There are so many festivals that happen over the summer in our city that I couldn't possibly include them all, so I've just highlighted a few favourites here.

But you'd be selling yourself short if you didn't take in some of the other amazing things Hamilton has to offer in the summer. Whether it's the classic Canadian pastime of paddling in a canoe, taking in a loud and thrilling historical re-enactment or hearing the crack of the bat as the home team sends one out of the park, there is so much to do in Hamilton in the summer.

Don't wait! Slip on your sandals, pack some snacks and drinks and get ready to fall in love with summer in the city all over again.

BATTLEFIELD HOUSE

The sound of cannons, the shouts of commanders, the rat-tat-tat of drums and the smell of gunpowder! Don't be alarmed, it's not conflict coming to our city, but the re-enactment of a pivotal battle in the War of 1812.

Battlefield House in Stoney Creek stands at the site of a battle between Canadian and American forces in June of 1813. This is where the much smaller Canadian force defeated a larger, better equipped American force after the Canadians had force marched from their fortifications at what is now Dundurn Castle in the middle of the night.

Every year, historical actors in period costumes

re-enact the battle using tools and weapons in the style of the period to the thrill of the gathered crowd.

Now known as the Battlefield House Museum and Park National Historic Site, the park features the original Gage family home where they were surrounded by the battle, along with walking trails and another historical building that was relocated there in 1999. The park also features a one hundred-foot-tall monument to peace and *Eagles Among Us,* a sculpture by Indigenous artist David General that is dedicated to peace and reconciliation.

The re-enactment happens every year in early June and takes place twice a day on the Saturday and Sunday of that weekend. The family-friendly event features a historical village, musical performers and games and entertainment from the period, as well as Indigenous programming.

On the Saturday afternoon before the re-enactment, there is also a narrated Great Peace Game of Haudenosaunee Lacrosse, with Haudenosaunee dancers and singers who perform right after the game.

During the re-enactment, the actors will be shooting (without ammunition) cannons and black powder muskets. There will also be shouting and drums as the two mock armies take their positions and recreate the famous battle. The evening re-enactments are followed by a fireworks display.

The event is always well attended, so be prepared for it to be busy. There is no parking on-site for the event, but there are free shuttle buses that run from the free parking lot at nearby St. John Henry Newman Catholic Secondary School. You can also catch the HSR route 05 or route 44 buses to be dropped off at the entrance to the park. Admission to the park that day is free.

As always when spending the day outdoors, be sure to bring a refillable water bottle, sunscreen and hats, or rain gear if the weather calls for it. Food can be purchased on-site from vendors, or you can pack a picnic. A blanket or folding chairs to sit on would also be a good idea.

You can find out more information and get tips for making the most of your day by going to www.hamilton.ca and searching "Battle of Stoney Creek."

FRANCOFEST

For three days in June, French-speaking Hamiltonians gather for FrancoFEST Hamilton, the largest Francophone celebration of arts and culture in the Niagara Region.

The event features musicians, songwriters, hip-hop performers, dancers and performers of all kinds, all in French and celebrating French-speaking culture. It takes place at Hamilton's Gage Park, making great use of the open lawns and the bandshell.

Every year there is a Family Zone that features performances such as circus performers, family-friendly music and a range of activities for kids young and old. In the past these have included bouncy castles, balloon sculptures and interactive drumming.

There are concessions on hand offering a variety of festival food, and picnic tables throughout so people can gather and catch up or meet new friends who love and appreciate Francophone arts and culture.

Previous performers have included Mélissa Ouimet, Wesli, Mi'gmafrica and ILAM. Performers are often award-winning and widely known in the Francophone community, both in Canada and around the world.

Gage Park is located at Gage Avenue and Main Street, and parking is just around back off Lawrence Road. Street parking is also available along Gage Avenue. The site is also fully serviced by HSR route 05.

The best part? The festival is free to attend and take part. Just bring a lawn chair or blanket and get ready to soak up the sun, and the sights and sounds of Francophone Ontario.

DUNDURN CASTLE HISTORIC KITCHEN GARDEN

Early summer is a time gardeners all over the city wait for. The leaves on the trees are fresh, flowers are blooming and the seeds planted just a few weeks ago are starting to sprout. The same is true for the gardeners at the Dundurn Castle Historic Kitchen Garden, just on a much bigger scale than your average backyard veggie grower.

The garden is situated on the east end of the Dundurn National Historic Site grounds, and features a two-acre area, fenced in with a historic-looking wooden stockade, filled with row after row of beautiful plants.

Here, the gardeners, often in period costumes,

tend to historic varieties of veggies and flowers, all grown as much as possible using period techniques from the 1850s. This means the plants are in long straight rows of a similar crop, with a thick layer of straw down to prevent weeds and moisture loss.

It also means that things like hotbeds are used. Small brick structures with a removable lid that use the heat from composting horse manure (courtesy of the Hamilton Police Service's mounted unit) to warm the soil and allow for planting much earlier in the year.

Harvesting and tending takes place throughout the day; however, the garden is generally only open in the afternoon on weekdays and on special occasions.

Staff grow over two hundred varieties of veggies, including period squash, beans and salad greens. One of the most popular parts of the garden is the large raspberry patch, where during the late summer juicy red raspberries are just calling out for you to pop one in your mouth – with permission from the staff of course.

A newer addition to the garden is Sophia's Garden, named after Dundurn Castle owner Allan MacNab's daughter. It is an area under a large shady maple tree that allows for sensory and free play for little ones. There is a table for the kids to sit at and eat snacks from home, and enjoy the summer breeze.

The garden is open from mid-May to mid-October for self-guided tours, educational programs and pre-booked tours. There is no charge for admission to the garden, and it is easily accessible with a large parking lot on the west side of the site, and the route 1 Burlington Transit bus running from downtown Hamilton and stopping just in front of the gardens. HSR route 08 also stops nearby at Dundurn Street North and York Boulevard.

HAMILTON CARDINALS

Ah, summertime, the smell of fresh-cut grass, the warm sun and the crack of a bat. Yes, summer for many means baseball, and you may be surprised to learn that you don't need to go all the way to Toronto to get your fix.

The Hamilton Cardinals are Hamilton's very own baseball team. They are members of a relatively unknown hundred-year-old league in Canada called the Intercounty Baseball League.

The team has been playing since 1958 and has only recently started to gain the popularity that long-term fans say they have always deserved.

The Cardinals play at Bernie Arbour Memorial

Stadium, located on Mohawk Road East between Upper Kenilworth Avenue, Limeridge Road East and Mountain Brow Boulevard. The stadium has been there since 1970 when it was built and named after a former police sergeant who had led the Hamilton Police Amateur Athletic Association for eighteen years.

There is on-site parking and street parking around the stadium, and you can also take the HSR if that's better for you. The stadium is served by routes 21 and 42.

The Cardinals play a 45–50 game schedule against teams from places like London, Kitchener, Barrie, Guelph and Welland. There are also a number of promotional nights on the roster, with different games and events held.

For instance, Friday is "beer batter" night, where a wheel is spun before the game to choose an opposing player's jersey number. If that player strikes out, it triggers happy hour pricing on beer for the rest of the inning.

More family-oriented offerings include Families on the Field, where you can bring your kids down to field level after the game to meet the players, and the Kids Run the Bases event, where kids get to run the bases on the field.

These fun events are driven by Eric Spearin,

who purchased the team in 2022 and immediately implemented a number of changes to improve the game day experience of fans. Other ideas have included beefing up the concessions to offer classic ballpark treats from Denninger's and Daniel Janetos Food Company. These changes have paid off, as the Cardinals have had some years since then with record attendance.

Those who attend Cardinal games share stories of a fun, welcoming, relaxed, family-friendly atmosphere – at significantly less cost and travel time than their higher profile cousins in Toronto.

CANOEING AT BINBROOK CONSERVATION AREA

What Canadian summer would be complete without at least one paddle in a canoe? Fortunately, in Hamilton we have an embarrassment of riches when it comes to getting into a people-powered watercraft.

Whether it's pushing through the lily pads at Cootes Paradise, navigating the narrow Christie Lake or squeezing your way up Grindstone Creek, there are plenty of places to paddle, but none of them really let you stretch out quite as much as the big reservoir at Binbrook Conservation Area.

Binbrook is a bit of an anomaly among conservation areas in the city in that it's not actually managed by the Hamilton Conservation Authority. Instead, it's a Niagara Peninsula Conservation Authority property, which means HCA passes aren't valid there. But don't let that stop you.

Binbrook's Lake Niapenco is wide and long and offers some great opportunities to spot wildlife along the shore as you paddle.

But the jewel in the crown is the island near the middle of the lake, which is complete with a picnic table and garbage can. It's the perfect location for a mid-paddle snack and rest before you tackle the rest of the lake heading down to the dam.

The best part? If you don't have a canoe, kayak or paddleboard of your own, you can rent one from the on-site rental company, Binbrook Wave Rentals, for a modest fee. They'll also supply life jackets, which are a must for even the most experienced paddler.

Finally, there is lots of great fishing in Lake Niapenco. While you're out paddling, be sure to take some time to cast a line and see what you can catch. Fishing regulations apply, and there are guidelines as to how often you can safely eat the fish in the lake, as there are in pretty much every body of water in southern Ontario.

Binbrook is open from 8:00 a.m. to 8:00 p.m. from May 1 to Thanksgiving Monday (and open sunrise to sunset after that) so there are plenty of opportunities to get on the water early before the wind picks up in the afternoon.

Once you're done with your paddle, you can relax on the sandy beach or have a picnic in one of the many grassy areas in the park and make the most of the rest of your day.

Fees are comparable to other conservation areas at $14.75 for a vehicle and driver, and $4.99 for each additional passenger, with a $30 maximum per vehicle.

The park is located at 5050 Harrison Road in Binbrook and there is no public transit service there.

Check out the Niagara Peninsula Conservation Authority's website at www.npca.ca and click on "Parks and Recreation" to get to the Conservation Areas page.

CANADA DAY FIREWORKS

Part of what makes fireworks so great is that they're not an everyday thing, and big, professional displays are even more rare. That's why opportunities to gather with friends and enjoy them are so special.

Every year on Canada Day – July 1 – the city puts on a day of celebrations at Bayfront Park at the corner of Bay Street North and Strachan Street West. The day features a wide range of entertainment for the whole family.

Activities for kids include inflatables (bouncy castles), face painting, balloon animals, giant life-sized games and stilt walkers. There are lots of things to do for grown-ups too, including musical performances, a huge range of food trucks and local variety performers such as magicians and ventriloquists. It's a great day to gather with friends and neighbours from across the city and celebrate what it is to be Canadian.

The day wouldn't be complete, however, without the big fireworks display.

On Canada Day, the sun tends to set at around 9:00 p.m., and by the time twilight has ended and it's fully dark, it will be about 9:45 p.m. or so. At 10:00 p.m. the action starts. From a barge in Hamilton Harbour, the fireworks light up the sky, along with musical accompaniment.

The event is easy to get to, with an HSR shuttle going from King Street in front of Jackson Square to the park every fifteen minutes starting mid-afternoon.

There is parking at Bayfront Park, but it fills up quickly. If you choose to park in the surrounding neighbourhood, be prepared for a bit of a hike to the best firework-viewing spots. There is a path that runs across the top of the park (directly west from the Bay and Strachan intersection). When you reach the lookout, there is a walkway to the left, or stairs on either side of the lookout.

As always for a big event, be sure to lock your

vehicle properly if parking nearby, and to keep all valuables out of sight.

Canada Day is a great day to celebrate the great country we live in, and a great day to catch the biggest fireworks display of the year. Grab your lawn chairs or picnic blanket and head down to Bayfront Park.

IT'S YOUR FESTIVAL

It's Canada Day long weekend, and you're itching to celebrate. But a barbeque seems kind of boring and none of your friends invited you to the cottage; this is the year to head to Gage Park for It's Your Festival!

Every year, this free and fun event brings great musical acts from across Canada and around the world to the bandshell at Gage Park, along with a number of smaller stages.

Headliners in the past have included Canadian acts like The Pursuit of Happiness, The Box and Big Sugar, along with international talent like Usher. The main stage runs Friday and Saturday evenings until late and ends a little earlier on Sunday evening. Get there early to stake out a spot with your blanket and chairs on the lawn, or snag a table at the beer garden set right next to the main stage.

The festival also features three other stages, including a New Music Expo that features up-and-coming new bands you may not have heard, and likely won't hear at other big festivals. Many successful Hamilton bands started their careers on this stage. The stage is usually set up among the pine trees just west of the greenhouse.

Across the park, you'll find the Lloyd A. Turner Children's Stage, featuring performances geared toward younger attendees. And, of course, it wouldn't be the community festival it is without the Community Stage, featuring cultural performances from Hamiltonian groups who hail from all over the world.

If you're hungry, there is always a long line of food trucks at the event to satisfy any craving, and you'll find a wide range of vendors of all sorts of goods in the vendor area. The event also features my family's favourite part: A midway with rides and classic games of chance for everyone to enjoy.

Gage Park is located at Gage Avenue and Main Street East, and there is ample parking just around back off Lawrence Road, or street parking also available along Gage, to the south of Main just west of the park. The site is also fully serviced by HSR route 05.

SUPIES

"I'm bored!" comes the refrain from so many kids over the summer. You're trying to keep a lock on screen time and want them to go outside and play, but "There's nothing to doooooo!"

Supies to the rescue! While the Supie program isn't unique to Hamilton, we may have the longest running program of this kind, started here over 115 years ago. Simply put, these are drop-in day programs that run in selected parks across the city, either every day or on specific days during the summer, which are staffed by older students.

Supies aren't babysitters, so if your child is too young to be at the park on their own you'll need to accompany them, but they do offer a whole range of activities for your kid to chase away the summer doldrums. Supies are also weather dependent, so if it's pouring rain, they likely won't be there.

Some days Supies will run circle games, other days there will be crafts or other activities in the park. Participants gather at picnic tables in the shade to learn new ways of having fun and make friends with neighbourhood kids that they may not have met yet.

The best part? It's all free. There is no cost for participation or even for craft supplies. The Supies come ready for fun and bring everything they need with them every day.

Who are these magical people you may ask? For the most part they are high school and university students who are hired by the city by the dozens in early spring every year. Whoever they are, they bring the fun to your local park.

The city's website (go to www.hamilton.ca and search "Supie") will tell you which park has full-time Supies – which run from 10:30 a.m. to 3:30 p.m. every day – and which ones have pop-ups one morning or afternoon a week.

Check out when they'll be there and send your kids to the park for some good healthy fun outside in the sun!

HAMILTON FRINGE FESTIVAL

At the height of summer, the city fills with the sounds and sights of independent theatre, as venues big and small across the city host audiences excited to catch the next hit show before it makes the big time.

That's right, it's the Hamilton Fringe Festival, a twelve-day extravaganza of live theatre that happens each July. Fifty theatre companies put on over 350 shows at venues across the city, giving you not only a chance to see independent theatre at it's best, but also the chance to step into some theatre spaces you might not normally go to.

The festival features a wide range of performance styles, including plays, musicals, puppetry, one-person shows, sketch comedy, improv, dance and magic shows. You're always sure to discover something new with the purchase of a fringe button that entitles you to low-cost tickets for every performance.

Fringe theatre is a tradition that started in Scotland in 1947 and has since spread around the world. Hamilton's festival has some things in common with the other festivals across Canada. For one, shows are not chosen by an artistic director or jury. Instead, performance slots are awarded by lottery, in order to allow everyone an equal chance at performing.

Also, when you purchase a ticket, you know that 100 percent of the proceeds from the show are going to the artists. For a small, or just starting, theatre company, mounting a successful Fringe production can be just the financial shot in the arm they need to take on their next project or to take the show to bigger theatres and audiences.

That said, fifty shows can be a lot to try and sort out, so it's a good idea to have a good read through the online program, and to look for reviews in local publications like the *Hamilton Spectator* and *Hamilton City Magazine* online. Also be sure to ask other theatre-loving friends what they've seen and what they've enjoyed.

All shows are general admission (there is no reserved seating) and shows always start on time, so be sure to show up ten minutes early to the venue to ensure you get a good seat.

Venues in the past have included The Westdale theatre, The Staircase theatre, Mills Hardware and Theatre Aquarius, but the venues shift slightly from year to year, so be sure to check online for the latest.

Check out www.hftco.ca for more details, for the program and for tickets. And who knows, maybe this will be the year you see the show that will let you say, "I saw them before they made it big!"

GRAND RIVER CHAMPION OF CHAMPIONS POWWOW

If the thrill of drumming, the bright colours of regalia and a centuries-old tradition of dancing and singing is your thing, you won't want to miss the Grand River Champion of Champions Powwow.

This traditional dance competition takes place every year on the fourth weekend in July at the Ohsweken Speedway on the Six Nations of the Grand River reserve. You'll see internationally ranked dancers performing their very best for an audience that comes from all over Canada and the United States to witness the spectacle.

The powwow has been running since 1980 and is, and has always been, run entirely by volunteers.

Generous sponsors support the work of the organizing committee, and all are welcome to attend.

Dancing is accompanied by singing and drumming in a traditional Indigenous style, and the prize money that dancers can be awarded is substantial. It's enough to draw the best of the best from across North America.

The event takes place in the afternoon and evening, with dancing continuing until after dark under the bright lights of the speedway. There are also over thirty food vendors selling a wide range of delicious treats and meals, and over a hundred craft vendors for gifts and items such as leatherwork, beadwork and jewellery.

Powwows are a time of celebration, building relationships and respect, and this one in particular can get quite busy. It's a good idea to arrive early to take advantage of seating in the stands, or bring a camp chair so you'll have somewhere to sit if the stands are full.

Visitors are also reminded to listen carefully to the master of ceremonies for cues for when to stand or remain silent out of respect. Also, please note that no drugs or alcohol of any kind are permitted at the event.

Photography is permitted, and again the MC will let you know when it's not appropriate to take photographs. If taking a photo of a dancer who is not performing at the time, you should always ask their permission.

No pets are allowed at the event except for guide dogs for the blind and visually impaired.

Gates open at 10:00 a.m. on Saturday and Sunday, with the powwow grand entry at noon on both days and 7:00 p.m. Saturday evening.

The route 15 GO Transit bus will take you there from McMaster Innovation Park, or it's a thirty-minute drive from downtown Hamilton to the speedway. Parking is free, and admission to the powwow is $15 for adults and teens, and $5 for children under 12. There is a two-day pass for $25.

For more information, and everything you need to plan your visit, head to www.grpowwow.ca.

CAMPING AT VALENS LAKE

Summertime for a lot of people means splashing in a lake, going for walks in the forest and big roaring bonfires. Did you know that you can get all three, right within the Hamilton city limits?

Valens Lake Conservation Area is this magical location, featuring dozens of kilometres of hiking trails, a sandy beach and a lake for canoeing and fishing. And the best part? You can camp there.

Valens Lake campground is one of the only year-round camping spots in southwest Ontario, so if you're feeling brave you can even camp there in the dead of winter, but summer and autumn are when this area really shines.

The campground boasts 225 campsites, with 125 of them featuring electric outlets and water hookups. For the "in the city but in the wilderness" experience, there are also six walk-in sites easily accessible with a short hike of less than a kilometre.

The campsites are organized into radio-free and regular, with the radio-free sites not allowing any amplified music for those who like their camping with a bit more peace and quiet. Valens is also 100 percent alcohol free all year round, so the rowdy parties that sometimes occur in campgrounds don't tend to happen. It is truly a family experience.

There are comfort stations featuring showers and flush toilets, and even a small camp store that sells ice cream, freezies, cold pop and a variety of last-minute camping needs like sunscreen and bug spray.

The campground is fully open and all sites are serviced from the May long weekend to Thanksgiving weekend inclusive.

For those who want to get outside, but don't want to sleep in a tent or RV, Valens also offers cabins for rent. You can sleep indoors and in comfort but still have a perfect view of the lake right outside your door. However, these cabins book up quickly, especially on long weekends, so if you're looking to rent one, it's a good idea to be online on the day bookings open.

Valens Lake is located on Regional Road 97, just a few minutes west of Highway 6. There is no transit nearby, but there is plenty of parking and room for vehicles and RVs.

You can learn more by going to www.conservationhamilton.ca and searching "Valens Lake Conservation Area."

DUNDAS CACTUS FESTIVAL

It's the middle of August, and the days are still hot, but the evenings are starting to cool off. You want to squeeze as much out of the rest of summer as you can, but how to do it?

Your first stop should be at the intriguingly named Dundas Cactus Festival.

Not a festival celebrating cactus at all, rather it was named by the organizers in 1975 as a tribute to a local greenhouse that excelled at growing these spiky little succulents.

Now? It's a three-day extravaganza of food, music and entertainment for the whole family. The event features musicians and a variety of other performers across three stages stretching the length of King Street through downtown Dundas.

Admission is free, and the kids will be sure to enjoy the Fortinos Family Fun Zone. This area includes a stage with children's performers, costumed characters, inflatables (bouncy castles), face painting and a twice-a-day teddy bear parade.

For adults, there are plenty of outstanding performers, with a strong focus on local talent. Musicians span the range of styles from pop tribute bands to local blues, rock and jazz musicians.

The festival also features twice daily bouts from Hamilton Pro Wrestling. Catch the high-flying action and drama from the ring on King Street between Main and Ogilvie.

If you're feeling brave, you can match your wits against the (very small) escape rooms on-site. These are free, and run all evening on Friday, all day on Saturday and until mid-afternoon on Sunday.

And if it's thrills you want, you won't want to miss the BMX display, with riders testing a challenging course of jumps and half-pipes. The Jagger Big Air Show runs throughout the festival.

On top of all this is a marketplace along King Street with over 120 vendors selling artwork, craft items and a range of other goods.

Parking is, to be honest, not great in downtown

Dundas. There is street parking in the neighbourhoods around the festival, but carpooling or public transit are probably your best bet. The festival is served by the HSR route 05 bus that detours around the event for its route.

Check out all the details on the website at www.dundascactusfestival.ca to learn more, and get ready to spend the weekend in the sun.

FESTIVAL OF FRIENDS

I might have mentioned that summer in Hamilton is all about festivals, and this continues with the Festival of Friends. This is one of the two largest free outdoor music festivals in Hamilton and it takes place every year on the Civic Holiday long weekend in August at Gage Park, rain or shine.

A thoroughly family-friendly event, the Festival of Friends features a large vendor area – which includes everything from toys to vintage clothing – along with face painters and balloon artists, a midway with games and rides, and three music stages. There are also a number of food trucks on-site with a broad range of styles of food available, from traditional carnie fare such as twisted potatoes to more unusual items like churros and desserts from around the world.

The main draw, though, is the music. Festival of Friends seems to outdo itself every year with big-name acts on the main stage at the historic bandshell, mainly from the '70s, '80s and '90s, headlining on Saturday night. Acts in the past have included everyone from perennial favourite David Wilcox to Randy Bachman and Gord Downie, to international stars such as the Village People.

The rest of the weekend the focus is strongly on local acts. This festival is also often a venue where up-and-coming bands can play for big audiences for the first time.

On Saturday and Sunday, the music runs from noon until 11:00 p.m., providing plenty of slots for a wide range of performers.

Across the park from the main stage is the children's area, where dynamic children's performers have kids singing, dancing, clapping and moving to tunes geared just for them.

The festival is a long-running tradition in Hamilton, going back to 1976. Despite a brief relocation to Ancaster in the mid-2010s, heading down to Gage Park for an August afternoon of fun and music has been part of many Hamiltonians' summers for as long as they can remember.

Gage Park is located at the corner of Gage Avenue and Main Street and can be accessed easily by HSR routes 01 and 05, or you can park behind the park just off of Lawrence Road (just be sure not to turn into the tennis club parking lot).

WINONA PEACH FESTIVAL

There's nothing better on a hot August day than biting into a fresh juicy peach, right from the tree. But what if you could get that much peach flavour and so much more? That's where the Winona Peach Festival comes in.

Started in 1967 as a celebration of Canada's centennial, the festival has been running ever since. It takes place over the second last weekend of August, and features three fantastic days of vendors, midway rides and games, a pageant and oh so many peaches.

The event starts with a walk through the midway featuring a wide range of games and rides for all ages. Bring some cash and be prepared to buy some tickets for the rides, as it will have all the ones you fondly remember from when you were a kid.

If your kids are into winning prizes, you won't want to miss the fish pond, where young people can fish for a prize in a large container of water. Where else can you be guaranteed a prize for $3?

There is also a large arts and crafts area with over eighty-five vendors from all around Ontario showing their unique and beautiful handiwork.

Of course, no festival like this would be complete without live entertainment, and the Peach Festival has two stages – one for children and one for everyone – that feature local performers and Winona favourites.

On Sunday night at the main stage, the winning ticket is drawn for the 50/50 lottery. Tickets are sold all weekend, and you can also purchase tickets outside of the fair at local vendors.

Then there's the food court area – a range of vendors sell a wide variety of food and snacks, but the highlight is always the peaches. Peach cobbler, peach sundaes, peach smoothies, peach salsa and other peach-flavoured treats. Come hungry and be prepared to eat your fill.

Admission is free to the festival. Parking is

available nearby, and there is an express shuttle bus from Eastgate Square that goes directly to and from the festival if you'd rather park there. You can also reach Eastgate easily by HSR routes 01 or 05. The event takes place in Winona Park at 1328 Barton Street, Winona.

Check out www.winonapeach.com for more details and up-to-date information.

Plan to take a sweet, juicy bite out of the end of summer and attend the Winona Peach Festival.

FALL

Autumn isn't everyone's favourite season, but it should be. Is there ever a time when the air is as crisp, the skies are as blue and the temperature is as perfect? I didn't think so.

It's also a fantastic time to get out and enjoy the city. Some people will want to take in the autumn leaves on a walk to Dundas Peak, while others will take in a fall fair or cheer on Hamilton's football team against our oldest rival.

Fall has so much to offer. Put on your coziest sweater, grab that latte or hot chocolate and head out the door. The best Hamilton has to offer is waiting to be discovered by you.

LABOUR DAY CLASSIC

Hamilton is well known for being a scrappy city. Often overshadowed by our larger cousin just up the QEW, Hamilton has developed a finely honed sense of when people are looking down on us, and an eagerness to stand up for ourselves.

Sometimes this comes out in politics, or culture, or economics, but nowhere is it more true than the rivalry between the Hamilton Tiger-Cats and the Toronto Argonauts in the Canadian Football League.

For those uninitiated, Canadian football is a much faster game that relies more on passing than the version in the U.S. and is played on a longer field. These factors, combined with some interesting rule variations from the NFL, make for an exciting game that is often unpredictable. Last play wins and losses are common.

The Hamilton Tiger-Cats are also a storied franchise. The team was formed officially in 1950 when the Tigers (who had been around since 1869) merged with the Wildcats, and history was made.

The rivalry with Toronto has been around just as long, and that rivalry comes to a head every year with the football game known as the Labour Day Classic.

It's a game played Labour Day Monday every year when Toronto stalwarts make their way down the QEW to face a hyped-up Hamilton crowd chanting, "Argos Suck!" and the Ticats team cheer.

If you don't know, the team cheer is:

> Oskee wee-wee, Oskee wah-wah,
> Holy Mackinaw, Tigers eat 'em raw!

You'll certainly hear it game day, and will pick it up soon enough, led in the stands by Pigskin Pete, a crowd-encouraging figure similar to, but not quite a mascot. Games take place at Hamilton Stadium.

Tickets go quickly, so make sure to get them

early, or make friends with someone with season's tickets. Be prepared to wear black and gold and to make some noise. There are a number of concessions in the stadium selling food and drink, and outside food (especially alcohol) is strictly prohibited. Be prepared to go through a metal detector to get into the stadium.

The stadium is located on Cannon Street between Melrose and Balsam Avenues, and that area is very, very busy on game day.

For parking around the stadium, take advantage of a wonderful tradition where many residents in the Stipley neighbourhood offer up driveways and yards for parking for a fee. There are also a few official lots near the stadium, but at $25 a spot they're much more expensive than the average Stipley driveway. You can find the official lot information on the Ticat's website at www.ticats.ca. There is limited street parking in the area too.

The HSR runs shuttles to and from the game from Eastgate Square, Lime Ridge Mall and University Plaza, along with regular service routes along King and Cannon.

Every Hamiltonian should go to at least one Labour Day Classic in their lives. It's a wonderful tradition that brings the whole city together to cheer for our city's most cherished team.

SUPERCRAWL

Supercrawl is a three-day extravaganza featuring music, art, theatre, writing, fashion and more that happens the second weekend of September every year.

Started in 2009, the festival was born of the monthly art crawls that take place on the second Friday of the month along James Street North. During these events, artists line the streets to sell their art and street performers entertain crowds for tips.

Supercrawl takes the spirit of art crawl to its logical conclusion. Two stages of headline music acts bookend the event – one on James and King, the other at James and Murray – and feature big-name touring acts alongside popular local bands and artists.

Near the Murray Street stage is the Authors Tent, where writers from Hamilton and around southern Ontario come to read their works, be interviewed and sign books for eager readers.

To the south are rows and rows of artists and vendors selling everything from vintage clothing to records to paintings and prints, along with much more. This is a curated section, so you won't see quite the same wild mix you sometimes find at an art crawl, but you will find lots of wonderful arts and crafts.

In the midst of that are the art installations near the Armoury, where artists from around the world are invited to come and install a large-scale piece of street art. This can be anything from sculptures to video installations to interactive art that people can touch and feel and even take their photo with.

Watch for the theatre stage and the fashion tent as you walk along the street. You'll find the Family Zone, where all things youthful come alive, at the intersection of Wilson and James. That's followed by the food truck area just before the King Street stage.

You can walk the whole thing in half an hour,

but you'll miss a lot if you do. Plan to spend an afternoon or evening enjoying the installations, picking up a piece of art and taking in a show you won't see anywhere else.

The whole event is free, paid for by generous sponsors and various granting bodies including the City of Hamilton.

Supercrawl's lineup announcement happens every summer near the end of June; keep your eyes on social media, or on their website at www.supercrawl.ca.

Don't miss this fall tradition that attracts musicians, artists and attendees from all over to see the best of what Hamilton has to offer.

GRIFFIN HOUSE

If you've ever hiked the full Dundas Valley loop, then at some point you've seen the sign directing you to the historic Griffin House and maybe wondered what it was all about.

Well, I'm here to tell you that you should definitely make the trek up the hill on a Sunday afternoon in September and check out this fascinating slice of Hamilton history.

The home was built in 1827 and purchased in 1834 by Enerals and Priscilla Griffin. The Griffins were formerly enslaved people in the United States who escaped to Canada and freedom in the early 1800s.

As two of the earliest Black settlers in Hamilton, their homestead is an important part of the city's story. The house is a national historic site and is typical of the type of homes built at the time, but is a rare surviving example of that period's wooden architecture.

The family lived in the home and farmed the area around it for 150 years, until it was purchased by the Hamilton Conservation Authority and originally restored in the early '90s. At the time, over three thousand artifacts were discovered, some of which are displayed in the home.

Since 2022, the house has been under further restoration, with plans to restore the foundation and add ramps to make the building accessible, among other elements.

The house is located at 733 Mineral Springs Road, with only accessible parking on-site. For everyone else there is parking at the Hermitage just up the road. The property is (when construction isn't being done) open from 1:00 p.m. to 4:00 p.m. on Sundays from July to September. You can also reach the site from the Headwaters Trail in the Dundas Valley Conservation Area, which leads to the Griffin House trail just north of the Hermitage.

Please check the City of Hamilton's website to see the opening hours of the property, but even if it's not open when you go, there are historical plaques around the area, and you can see the place where some of Hamilton's first Black settlers lived, worked, raised a family and made their home.

TELLING TALES

They say that the best way to raise a lifelong reader is to start them young, but with such a huge range of children's books available, how can you figure out what your child will enjoy? Perhaps it would help if there was a way to take in a wide range of books and book-themed activities on a sunny day in an outdoor setting.

Telling Tales to the rescue! This early fall event happens every year in the Hendrie Park section of the Royal Botanical Gardens, and features authors, crafts, kids' activities and five stages of fun for kids of all ages. It's the largest children's book festival in Canada.

Every year the festival features readings from authors from across Canada that will captivate and delight your child. The books presented range from picture books for the little ones all the way up to the latest in young adult fiction.

There is also a good selection of nonfiction authors for the kids who like to just stick to the facts.

As well as the stages, there are wandering performers portraying beloved children's book characters, interactive walks and puppet shows, and if the kids get a little wild, you can take them for a run on one of the big lawns in Hendrie Park.

The event also features vendor tables where you can buy some fun things for the kids, and book tables that feature books from every presenter at the festival.

Dates vary slightly each year, so check www.tellingtales.org for the most up-to-date details. There you can also find the schedule of author appearances, a list of vendors who will be on-site and details for accessing the event. (Spoiler: Access is via the RBG main building, through a really cool tunnel.)

The event is free, and although the RBG has a big parking lot, it fills up quickly. Either get there early or be prepared to hike from any overflow lot they have designated. You can also reach the event via the route 1 Burlington Transit bus (which stops in downtown Hamilton with several connection points with the HSR), which stops essentially in front of the main building.

ROCKTON WORLD'S FAIR

Sometimes small, local events get very popular and take on big aspirations. People want to celebrate them and tell the whole world how great they are. Some of our local fall agricultural fairs are no exception, and none more so than the legendary Rockton World's Fair.

Rockton is a small village nestled along Highway 8, but every Thanksgiving weekend, the Rockton fairgrounds is a bustling hub of activity, with people coming from all over southern Ontario to celebrate the fall and Hamilton's agricultural heritage.

The fair has been running since 1853, first as

the Beverly Township Agricultural Show, and then the Rockton Fair. But in 1878, in a meeting to discuss the success of that year's event, it was decided that no other country fair in the area could measure up, and it was half-jokingly suggested it be renamed the World's Fair. The *Hamilton Spectator* newspaper ran with that as the headline the next morning, and the rest is history.

The fair is, in fact, pretty spectacular. Every year, there is a huge range of activities and things to see, including agricultural competitions for cattle, hogs, horses and sheep, as well as prize corn and grains. There is also a substantial midway featuring popular rides and games, and a wide range of shows, from horse show jumping to a giant pumpkin competition.

Friday, Saturday and Sunday evenings also feature the very popular demolition derby, where people enter their old beaten up (and often reinforced) cars into a competition to try and smash everyone else's vehicles into smithereens by crashing into them. The last car still running is the winner.

There is also a pie-eating contest, and the ever-popular talent show on Monday evening, where aspiring stars can strut their stuff for an enthusiastic audience.

Your admission entitles you to park on the

grounds, and family and weekend passes are available.

The fairgrounds are located on Old Highway 8 (just off of Highway 8) in Rockton, just northwest of Waterdown. Taking Highway 5 westbound to Highway 8 and watching for the signs is the easiest route to drive there. In a testament to the wide popularity of the event, the HSR also offers a free shuttle to the fair from various points in the city.

Plan to take in at least one fall fair this autumn, to celebrate Hamilton's long history of agricultural achievement. Why not make it the Rockton World's Fair?

GAGE PARK FALL GARDEN AND MUM SHOW

Every autumn, most people start thinking about putting their gardens to bed and getting ready for a fairly plant-free winter. Not so the good people in the horticultural department at Gage Park. Their thoughts turn instead to capping off the gardening year with a dazzling display.

The Gage Park Fall Garden and Mum Show happens every fall in the first couple of weeks of October, and features a fantastic display of bright and beautiful blooms inside the spacious greenhouse in Gage Park.

The show, affectionately called the "mum show," has been running since 1920, and is a labour of love for City of Hamilton horticultural staff who grow and arrange the blooming plants to perfection. The show features over two hundred different varieties of chrysanthemums and over one hundred thousand blooms. It's a spectacular sight.

The greenhouse is a wonderful place to visit year-round, especially in the dead of winter with its tropical plants, warmth and strategically located seating areas. It is always a great place to spend an afternoon or even do some "work from home."

That said, the mum show is where it really comes into its own.

Admissions for the show vary from year to year but are generally $10 for adults, with discounts for seniors, children and families.

While you're at Gage Park, fall is also a great time to head over to the area just to the east of the greenhouse and check out the Children's Garden, which by then will be in full harvest.

Parking is free and is available in the lot off of Lawrence Road, or there is bus service via HSR route 05 to various stops around the perimeter of the park. Route 01 also stops at the eastern edge of the park coming westbound.

Plan to make the annual Gage Park mum show part of your autumn experience. The blooms are waiting for you!

DUNDAS PEAK

If fall colours are your thing, Hamilton has an embarrassment of riches in terms of places to go and see the bright reds, oranges and yellows of the changing leaves. However, the peak experience might be at Dundas Peak.

This incredibly popular (for all the right reasons) hike winds its way from the Tew Falls access point in Dundas along the side of the escarpment to a fantastic lookout with perfect views of the entire Dundas Valley.

The lookout itself is protected by an attractive, wrought-iron-looking fence, which won't detract from your selfie game at all while keeping little ones and dogs safe.

The catch is that the hike is now so popular that during peak season you must reserve a spot in advance at the Hamilton Conservation Authority website. That reservation entitles you to a two-hour window in which to enjoy the hike. Don't worry, that will give you plenty of time to take all the photos you can.

The cost to register for the hike is $10 on the HCA website, with a parking cost of $11 per vehicle and $5 per occupant. If you have an HCA pass, the only cost is the reservation fee.

Be sure to book well in advance (at least a couple of days) because this hike fills up quickly. Day-of bookings are only possible either very early or quite late in the season. For the best leaf show, you'll need to plan ahead.

Like all hikes in nature, you should bring some water in a reusable container and a snack, as well as sunscreen and/or bug spray depending on the conditions. Always wear sturdy shoes and bring a small first aid kit or a couple of adhesive bandages for skinned knees.

There are no garbage cans along the route, so be prepared to pack out what you pack in.

Finally, if you have a pair of binoculars, they will be good for spotting the fall migration southward of raptors such as red-tailed hawks and turkey vultures who will be on the move this time of year as well.

For more information, head to the Hamilton Conservation Area website, www.conservationhamilton.ca.

CEMETERY TOUR

Hamilton's long and often colourful history is written in stone; literally in the stones that indicate the resting places of the long departed in Hamilton's oldest cemetery, Hamilton Cemetery on York Boulevard.

While wandering through the cemetery and seeing the names and dates can be a fascinating afternoon for a history buff, if you really want to do a deep dive you'll need to take a tour from a knowledgeable historian.

Fortunately, that's easy to do, as the City of Hamilton offers tours every second and fourth Sunday of the month at 10:00 a.m., from May through November.

Tours include topics such as women of Hamilton, historic battles, the War of 1812, the cholera epidemic, naval battles and the McQuesten family. Guides blend engaging storytelling with facts and figures to paint a complete picture of life during the time, and the context of the stones being viewed.

Tours are generally between one and two hours long and run rain or shine. Participants are asked to dress for the weather, bring a bottle of water (reusable please!) and wear good walking shoes; the ground in the cemetery can be a little uneven.

For those who are looking for a more personal experience, you can also book private tours for small groups through the city. Both private and public tours are free of charge, but the private tours are subject to staff availability.

As always, participants are asked to observe proper cemetery etiquette. This is a place where the dead have been laid to rest, and it is an active cemetery where people still come to be with their loved ones. As such, you are asked to keep noise to a minimum, stay on the roadway where possible, and keep pets on a leash and clean up after them at all times.

More information about Hamilton Cemetery

and the tours can be found by going to www.hamilton.ca and searching “Historical Walking Tours.”

HAMILTON ASSOCIATION FOR THE ADVANCEMENT OF LITERATURE, SCIENCE AND ART (HAALSA)

Sometimes the fall means cold, rainy nights, where you want something to do that isn't outdoors. Sometimes you also want to spend some time with curious people with a thirst for knowledge and learning about our big, increasingly complex world.

What if I told you that there is a lecture series in Hamilton that has been providing just that since before Canada was a country?

The Hamilton Association for the Advancement of Literature, Science and Art (also known as the Hamilton Association or HAALSA) sprang from the Hamilton Scientific Association in 1857, founded in part by the legendary explorer John

Rae. Since then it has been offering talks every year by scientists, explorers, artists and thinkers on the widest range of topics you can imagine.

Just in the past few years, lecture subjects have ranged from Antarctic exploration to the wonders of deep space, the history of the Royal Botanical Gardens and the state of comic books and illustration in Canada. There is truly something for everyone.

There are eight or nine lectures a year, and they currently take place in room 1A1 at the Ewart Angus Centre in the McMaster University Health Sciences Centre. Lectures are generally held the first or second Saturday of the month and start at 7:30 p.m.

Parking, as with all McMaster events, is tricky, but you can enter from Main Street and choose a lot near the south end of the campus. Or you can catch either HSR route 01 or 05 and walk the short distance from the University at Life Sciences stop to the Health Sciences Centre.

And the cost? Nothing. Free as the air, but they do accept donations if you are so inclined. In fact, if you enjoy your lecture, you might consider becoming a member of the Association and having a say in how it's run at a subsequent Annual General Meeting.

You can find everything you need to know at www.haalsa.org, including the list of upcoming lectures.

HAMILTON PHILHARMONIC ORCHESTRA (HPO)

There is a musical treasure trove in Hamilton of stories in song going back hundreds of years, and while many Hamiltonians know about it, I'm always surprised at how many have never gone to see it.

I'm referring, of course, to the Hamilton Philharmonic Orchestra.

The HPO has been a staple of the city's music scene for 140 years, making it one of the oldest cultural institutions in the city.

Mainstage performances run from September to June and feature a captivating mix of favourites and newer works. Along with performances of historical and serious modern classical pieces, the HPO also features performances of modern orchestral work such as film scores and even video game scores. These can be a great way to introduce young people to the thrill and energy of live orchestral music.

If you want to learn more about the piece you are about to hear, come early for the pre-show chat, where an expert will explain the story and history behind the pieces being played and give you some context for what the orchestra will be playing that day.

For those who would like to go even deeper, the Talk and Tea series features talks from various HPO members about works featured in that season's performances, with background stories and information. You'll even get some insight into the rehearsal process and how the orchestra prepares for the big night.

Finally, there are also performances of smaller ensembles from the orchestra in public settings like the Hamilton Farmers' Market, Supercrawl and branches of the library. Be sure to check out their website for more information.

The mainstage performances are in the acoustically wonderful First Ontario Concert Hall at 1 Summers Lane, directly across from City Hall.

There is ample parking in the underground garage adjacent to the venue, along with frequent bus service from all over the city at the Frank A. Cooke Transit Terminal next door.

Tickets can be had for single shows, or you can purchase a subscription package for the season, allowing you to attend a certain number of performances that you choose. More details are available at www.hpo.org, along with a great section on what to expect the day of performances.

Get ready to steep yourself in 140 years of history and musical excellence when you attend a performance of the HPO.

GRINDSTONE CREEK WALK

One of the great joys of living in Hamilton and Burlington in the late fall is a hike at Grindstone Creek.

The colours of the leaves are still hanging on, migrating birds are moving through and animals are getting ready to bed down for the winter.

Start at Cherry Hill Gate just across and down from the Royal Botanical Gardens' main building. Parking is available for a fee, or it's free if you have an RBG membership, so plan to spend a bit of time. You can also get there by the route 1 Burlington Transit bus, which stops in downtown Hamilton.

Head down the hill toward the wetland of

Grindstone Creek. Along the way you'll be descending into a valley of mixed deciduous (not evergreen) forest. Animals to look out for include chipmunks, American red squirrels, chickadees, hairy woodpeckers, nuthatches, cardinals and the occasional rabbit or raccoon.

When you get to the bottom of the trail, you can head across the boardwalk or turn into the woods. It's the same loop either way, and you'll end up back where you started. Along the way there are some somewhat steep hills, a small bridge over the creek and a boardwalk over a wetland.

Wildlife you may see include swans, mallards, Canada geese and maybe even the muskrat family that lives near the main bridge. If you go early in the morning or at twilight, you may also catch sight of the occasional deer.

Watch for the bright red twigs of the dogwood trees, and if they have any berries left, keep an eye out for birds snacking. The black berries you see are from the invasive European buckthorn. The reason the berries are still there in the late autumn is that they tend to make birds sick; I wouldn't recommend eating them either.

However, there is plenty for the birds to eat naturally, and they don't need your help with offerings of seeds or bread. In fact, feeding the wildlife in the area is liable to get you a ticket from a bylaw enforcement officer. It's bad for the wildlife, and not great for you if you get a fine.

Once you've done the loop, consider heading down the long stretch of boardwalk toward where Grindstone Creek flows into Hamilton Harbour. The walk takes you past some excellent examples of creek restoration, and some lovely giant maple trees along the path. If you're lucky, you'll catch a glimpse of a beaver along the creek. You can certainly see its handiwork (toothy-work?) on some of the trees along the shore.

If you make it all the way to the bay, you'll see the rows of Christmas trees in the water that act as a natural barrier (put there by the RBG) to prevent invasive species from swimming upstream into this ecologically sensitive area.

This section of the trail is more of a "there and back" hike than a loop, so at some point you'll have to bid the woods and the creek farewell and head back to your vehicle or the bus stop at the top of the hill, but you'll do so having spent some time restoring yourself in some of the best nature Hamilton has to offer.

HOLIDAYS

The holiday season – while not technically a season like the other four – is a magical time, made more so by all of the amazing events in Hamilton. Cultures around the world celebrate the shift from the darkest days to the slow advance of spring in a wide variety of ways, and Hamilton is no different.

For some, a celebration of the solstice complete with fire dances and stilt walkers will be just the thing. Others would love to take in a theatre production. Still others would just like to count birds in their backyard.

As we close off the year of things to do in Hamilton, there are still a few things left to get you up and moving and exploring this fascinating city.

SANTA CLAUS PARADE

Late November in Hamilton sees the whole city getting into the Christmas spirit with the annual Santa Claus parade.

Kids young and old and their families line the route to see bands, colourful floats, local community groups and of course the big man himself at the end of it all on his sleigh.

Get ready to eat your body weight in mini candy canes and enjoy the sights and sounds of one of Hamilton's few remaining parades.

The route has changed a few times in the past few years, but for now has settled on a mountain route of heading north on Upper Sherman Avenue, west on Limeridge Road and into Lime Ridge Mall for the end of the parade.

Families are welcome to place lawn chairs and blankets anywhere along the route that they can find a spot. It's also always a good idea to bring a thermos of something hot to drink, blankets to cuddle under and something to distract the kids if they start to get tired from sitting too long.

Be sure your phone is charged, as there will be lots of opportunities for photos along the way.

The parade has been running on and off for fifty years now, with a brief break during the Covid-19 pandemic lockdowns, but now it's back better than ever. Like so many activities in Hamilton, the parade is run entirely by volunteers, who organize the event, build the three main floats (Santa, Mrs. Claus and Frosty the Snowman) and work the route on parade day ensuring everyone is safe.

The parade features appearances by the Hamilton Tiger-Cats cheerleaders, a number of dance and cheer teams, several marching bands, cultural groups, costumed characters and mascots and first responders, among many others.

The parade also collects donations for the food bank along the way, so be sure to bring a can or two of non-perishables if you're able.

The timing of the parade changes year to year,

but the event is promoted heavily in both the local media and on social media. As the day approaches, you'll be able to get all the information you need at www.hamiltonsantaparade.com.

Bundle up the whole family and enjoy this long-time Hamilton tradition!

THEATRE AQUARIUS

Hamilton is lucky to have a number of award-winning live theatres that regularly mount professional and semi-professional productions of both old favourites and groundbreaking new shows.

The granddaddy of them all though has to be Theatre Aquarius. Hamilton's largest theatre space is also home to a theatre company of the same name that has been packing houses for over fifty years.

The theatre company mounts a number of productions each year, and often showcases new works, including the type of bold, professional theatre that can be hard to find outside of Toronto.

Theatre Aquarius also specializes in musicals. Every holiday season, the theatre puts on a musical that is perfect for the whole family to enjoy together and is also a great way to introduce younger family members to the wonders of the theatre.

In fact, Theatre Aquarius is the home of the National Centre for New Musicals, a project that is run in cooperation with the Incite Foundation for the Arts. This program is dedicated to incubating a new wave of Canadian musical productions, and it is constantly developing works for production and debut at the theatre.

Theatre Aquarius also features a strong educational component in its programming, with a professional theatre school that works with young artists who have theatre career aspirations to build their skills in music, dance, acting and theatre-making.

The theatre also offers a range of classes for kids as young as grade two and three, where they can learn about the basics of acting and performance in a fun, supportive environment. It also offers adult musical theatre classes for those of us who have always dreamed of having our moment in the limelight.

There are lots of reasons to visit Theatre

Aquarius, whether a show, a musical or a class. Their season runs from fall to spring. Head to www.theatreaquarius.org to learn more.

CPKC HOLIDAY TRAIN

Every year the CPKC rail company decorates a train with festive lights, puts a full stage on one of the cars, invites popular musicians to perform and goes coast to coast, stopping at cities along the way. As it goes, it collects donations for local food banks and warms everyone who attends with that holiday spirit.

In Hamilton, the train rolls through in late November/early December and brings music and lights to the rail yard across from Gage Park.

The train is brightly lit and has music playing as it goes, and you can catch it at various places in the east end of the city as it rolls through.

When it pulls into the yard, crowds gather, bringing their non-perishable goods (which are appreciated but not required), to enjoy a free concert of holiday favourites.

Bring hot chocolate or another warm beverage in a thermos for the kids and get ready to get all festive.

Some notes for attending: Expect crowds. This is a very popular event and can be quite busy. Keep an eye on little ones that they don't run off. Parking is often an issue for this event. You could park in the Gage Park parking lot and walk over, or park on the street in the surrounding neighbourhood, but expect it to be busy and spots harder to find the later you arrive.

Meanwhile HSR route 05 goes right by the location and is an easy way to get there and back.

The event is free and open to all, and is a great night of celebration and fun.

As the train exits the city, people often gather on rail bridges and at crossings in the west end as the train goes into the Hunter Street tunnel and then out through the Kirkendall neighbourhood before heading to its next destination.

Last year the train collected 1.75 million pounds of food across Canada and the U.S., making this a holiday celebration that not only warms hearts, but fills bellies as well.

For timing and a list of artists, head to www.cpkcr.com/en/community/HolidayTrain.

WINTER PROGRAMMING AT RBG

Every winter, the Royal Botanical Gardens pulls out all the stops to welcome the season in true botanical style.

Indoors at the RBG Centre, you can find the holiday train exhibit: A large-scale train display that features Thomas the Tank Engine–themed trains along with other modern and historical models, all travelling around a forest-themed track. Children can wander in among and under the tracks and explore all the little surprises that have been hidden in the woodland setting.

For slightly older model train lovers, over at the Rock Garden there is also a fantastic display featuring a stylized version of the escarpment and the city below. This display features models of modern CP and CN engines, along with historical Toronto, Hamilton and Buffalo Railway trains. The display also features some amazing miniatures and is full of sights to explore.

Back at the RBG Centre, there are holiday-themed flower and plant displays throughout the building, especially in the Breezeway and the Mediterranean Garden. Traditionally, the Breezeway has featured a massive poinsettia show with plants with a range of colours for those who love this traditional holiday favourite, and the Mediterranean Garden is always a wonderful place to sit in the warmth of the greenhouse and enjoy the scents and sights of this jewel in the garden's crown.

Holiday-themed decorations and events happen in the Hendrie Park garden as well, which vary from year to year, but can include train rides, visits with Santa and evening light displays.

There is a big parking lot at the main RBG building, as well as a smaller one across the street at the Cherry Hill Gate entrance to Hendrie Park, but both can fill up during special events. Watch for signs about overflow parking if both lots are full. The garden is also accessible from the route 1 Burlington Transit bus, which stops in downtown

Hamilton at King and Bay and other spots on its way back to Burlington. See Burlington Transit's website for more details.

It all comes alive at the Royal Botanical Gardens every winter. Check out www.rbg.ca for admission prices and other details.

HAMILTON WINTER SOLSTICE FESTIVAL

On the longest, darkest night of the year, Hamilton's Corktown neighbourhood comes alive with music, light and fire at the annual Hamilton Winter Solstice Festival.

Originally conceived by sound artists in 2017, the festival has been running on and off (with a break for Covid-19) since then.

Each year, artists and winter enthusiasts gather in Corktown Park on December 21 at dusk for this welcoming festival, which features art installations from visual and sound artists, along with dancers and fire artists.

Visual installations dot the park, often projected

onto large screens and fabric. There are often also light sculptures made of twists and lengths of light rope and other forms of illumination. Sounds and music are also an important part of the festival, with sound artists weaving a haunting, often ethereal soundscape over the event with live performances.

Join the dancers and performers who come from the Red Tree Artists' Collective in the light parade that gathers everyone for the grand finale, the burning of the sculpture in the middle of the large grassy area of the park. Fire-spinning artists then work their magic as the papier mâché sculpture sends flames up to the sky and burns down to ash behind them.

The event finishes at 9:00 p.m., and you can head home for a hot chocolate to warm up.

Corktown Park is located at the corner of Forest and Ferguson Avenues in Corktown, and there is parking along Forest Avenue if you get there early enough. There is also street parking in the surrounding neighbourhood, but watch for no parking and permit-only parking signs. The park can also be reached from a variety of HSR routes along John Street, about a ten-minute walk to the west of the park. The event is free, but donations to keep the festival running are gladly accepted.

Make your longest night the brightest night of the year and plan to attend the Hamilton Winter Solstice Festival.

CHRISTMAS BIRD COUNT

Every year, on Boxing Day, birding enthusiasts from all over the Hamilton area get together and count birds. Not just any birds, but the birds that have chosen to overwinter in Hamilton rather than migrating further south.

The Hamilton Christmas Bird Count is one of the oldest in Canada, having been run continuously since 1921. It centres on a twenty-five-kilometre-wide circle around Dundurn Castle.

Christmas Bird Counts were started by the organization that would eventually form the National Audubon Society in the U.S. as a response to the extinction of the passenger pigeon. Hamilton joined shortly after and has been counting birds via the Hamilton Naturalists' Club (HNC) ever since.

Each year, participants sign up on the HNC website (www.hamiltonnature.org) and are assigned an area to cover. If your backyard falls in the study area, the count may be as simple as looking out your kitchen window regularly to see what species of birds are gathered there.

There isn't a lot of birding expertise required to join. You can join other birders and just walk around your neighbourhood in your assigned area looking up at the trees (watch your step!). There isn't a huge diversity of birds that overwinter here, so the identification isn't too challenging.

Also, with most people having a smartphone in their pockets, there are apps and tools that will help you identify all but the trickiest birds.

The data that is collected is very important to science, and researchers regularly ask the HNC not only for the more recent digital counts, but also for historical data that goes back a century. Scientists can then track trends and changes to bird populations over a long period of time, giving them a clearer picture of the impacts of habitat loss and climate change.

This year, instead of filling up on leftovers and watching another holiday movie, consider layering up to head outside and contribute to the century-old tradition in Hamilton of counting the feathered friends who make this city their home too.

Jason Allen has lived in Hamilton with his family for twenty years, where he has spent much of that time scouring the city for things to do and ways to keep his kids occupied. Jason has lived in Calgary, Guelph, Toronto, Buffalo, Los Angeles and Reno, and would trade any of them for Hamilton. Jason works as an outdoor educator and adult learning course designer and writes for local publications about the city and the environment. He lives in the west end with his wife, two adult sons and two cats.